Navigating Global Transition – A Journey for Graduates

GRADUATE PLANNER

JENI WARD & KATH WILLIAMS

First Edition 2024

© COPYRIGHT INTERWOVEN 2024

All rights reserved. No part of this publication may be reproduced, stored in or introduced into a
Retrieval system; or be transmitted, in any form, or by any means (electronic, mechanical, photocopying, recording or otherwise) without the prior written permission of the publisher. This book is sold, subject to the condition that is shall not by way or trade or otherwise, be lent, resold hired out, or otherwise circulate without the publisher's prior consent, in any form of binding or cover other than that in which it is published and without a similar condition, including this   condition, being imposed on the subsequent purchaser.

ISBN paperback: 978-0-6457886-0-0

This edition was published in Aberfoyle Park by Mission Interlink in April 2024

Illustrations by:
River by Emma Elliot page 10
Artwork © Lorien Illustrations 2017. www.lorien-illustrations.com.
Typesetting by: Kath Williams
Cover layout by Kath Williams

Forward

When big changes in life hit, life gets overwhelming. There is a flood of unfamiliarity, and in the midst of that chaos we have to make decisions – often life-changing decisions. These seasons of transition are stressful, uncomfortable, and quite often turning points we'll look back on. I don't know about you, but I've often wished someone could just tell me what to do. Not make all my decisions for me, but just make it a bit easier! Calm the chaos, make order from the maelstrom of emotions and overwhelm.

In nearly twenty years working with teens and twenty-somethings from around the world who grew up outside their passport countries, I have heard hundreds of stories. Stories of their lives, their joys, their struggles, their journeys, their successes. One thing almost all of them had in common was that one of their most difficult seasons of change was finishing high school. The most difficult of all? Moving to live in their passport country. For a good chunk of TCKs, these two experiences overlap. No, they don't just overlap – they collide.

In the midst of the emotional and practical chaos of such a big season of transition, we can't keep track of everything. That is why this book is so important. It provides a comprehensive framework to scaffold one of the most difficult experiences of TCK life: finishing high school and moving away.

There are things in this book you will no doubt think are obvious. Great! This workbook will remind you to get working on them – and perhaps earlier than you would on your own. It paces out all the aspects of leaving well so you have time to fit everything in. Most importantly, it doesn't stop when you wave goodbye and get on that plane but continues with you into that first week after arriving, when all is chaos. It checks in with you a few months later, and guides you through that whole first year.

Seasons of transition are stressful. We often choose to tune out, turn off, ignore the stress and hope it goes away. Processing our stress is much more valuable, but it can feel so hard to do. The Graduate Transition Planner makes it easy. You still have to show up and do the work, but the steps have been laid out for you – all you need do is follow. What a gift.

I hope you embrace this gift: not only the book you are reading, but this whole season of life. As you process everything you go through, I hope you find peace in knowing others have trod this path ahead of you. You're entering a time of life that can be stressful, but you aren't alone in it.

Tanya Crossman
Author of Misunderstood: The Impact of Growing Up Overseas in the 21st Century

Navigating Global Transition: A journey for Graduates

Acknowledgements

Many thanks to all of those who have contributed; Mission Interlink and Interserve Australia for giving us the margin to make this collaboration possible. Also, to our families who have supported, encouraged, and provided childcare. We also want to thank all those people that work alongside TCKS.

Contents

About us	7
Introduction	8
Mood Tracker	9
Reflection Introduction	9
The River	10
Important dates & Birthdays	12
12 Months Ahead	**14**
Photo Scavenger Hunt	18
Pictures of where you live	19
9 Months Ahead	**20**
Pictures of your favourite restaurants	24
Pictures of important people in your life	25
6 Months Ahead	**26**
Write out your favourite phrases or slang from your country	30
Pictures of your favourite spots	31
3 Months Ahead	**32**
Make a packaging collage of your favourite labels	36
Recipes of your favourite food	37
2 Months Ahead	**38**
Pictures of your friends	43
1 Month Ahead	**44**
A copy of currency	48
Pictures of iconic/comical signs/Cultural things	49
1 Week Ahead	**50**
Create a map of where you currently live ?	54
Collect photos of the people you want to remember	55
Travel	**56**
World Map Colour in Page	59
1 Week After	**60**
1 Month After	**64**
Wreck this page	68
Photos of family before and after	69
3 Months After	**70**
Create a map of your new location	74
Photos of life at the moment and how you feel about it.	75
6 Months After	**76**
Favourite new restaurants and food	80
Wreck this page	81
9 Months After	**82**
Wreck this page	87
12 Months After	**88**
Favourite new phrases and slang	92
Favourite places	93
Glossary	94
Resources	95

About us

INTERWOVEN

Interwoven is a Missions Interlink Ministry, created through a partnership of dedicated workers with a passion for nurturing Third Culture Kids, ensuring their physical, spiritual, and mental well-being on the field. Our primary mission is to develop resources that directly engage Third Culture Kids. Additionally, we aim to support and provide valuable resources to those who work with and care for them.

KATH WILLIAMS (ISV AUSTRALIA)

Kath is a dedicated and professional social worker with a profound passion for supporting Third Culture Kids (TCKs) in their growth and development. Currently, she works with TCKs through two mission organizations in Australia. Kath is the co-author of "Navigating a Global Transition Again: A Journey of Faith" and "Thongs or Flip Flops: A Book for Aussie TCKs."

With 20 years of experience working with children and teens, Kath's diverse background includes work with Indigenous communities, foster children, and community camp-sites. She spent two years in Cambodia, where she contributed to the student support team at Hope International School and volunteered with middle and high school students at a local international church youth group.

Outside of her professional life, Kath enjoys going out for coffee and food with friends, exploring with her camera, visiting zoos, reading, listening to music, and traveling as much as she can.

JENI WARD (SIM AUSTRALIA)

Jeni Ward is a Third Culture Kid (TCK) whose journey has taken her across diverse landscapes including Ethiopia, South Sudan, Canada, and Australia. With over 13 years of experience in cross-cultural ministry, Jeni has dedicated her life to understanding and bridging the gaps between different cultures. As a lifelong learner, she is passionate about walking alongside other TCKs, offering guidance, support, and a deep sense of community.

As a founding member of Interwoven, an organization dedicated to developing materials and resources for TCKs (and the producer of this book). Through her work with Interwoven, she has been instrumental in creating resources that address the unique challenges and opportunities that come with a multicultural upbringing. These include God in the Mess and God in the Cracks. As well as co-authoring "Navigating a Global Transition Again: A Journey of Faith" All this together with Kath Williams. Check these great resources out at https://www.interwovenglobal.com .

Her commitment to this cause reflects not just in her professional life, but also in her everyday interactions, where she continuously seeks to connect, inspire, and empower those around her through coaching and debriefing.

Introduction

Dear Graduate,

As you enter your final year, here is a tool to help you prepare for the big changes to come in your life. There may be some hard moments but there will be some things to celebrate as well. This planner can help you ask questions and seek out support as you enter the next stage of life as you prepare to leave and as you enter your new country.

This is what each section has:
-Practical- This is where you can think through questions in regard to the move and make some decisions on the next step to take.
-Heart- Is intended for you to share with someone how you are feeling about the move and discuss them.
-Reflection-
-Thoughts and Plans- Give you an option to write down any plans or thoughts that you would like to process as you go along this journey.
-To do list- is for you to write down things you may need to accomplish that month.
-Mood Tracker- Is to track how you are going emotional.
Activities in which you can do.
-Wreck this Journal Page- This is an opportunity to create it as unique as you that means you can add photos, deface the page, colour outside. It is up to you.
-Don't be limited if you run out of space just add more pages.
-Do it in your own time there is no race.
-Feel free to read ahead and think about what is coming.
-Hash-tag us if you want in some of your pictures at #interwoven
- Bridging person- Is some one from your passport country who you can walk alongside with. Ask those questions you want too.

This is your planner make it your own.

You can walk through this planner by yourself, alongside your family or with your classmates. We recommend finding a bridging person in the country you are moving too. This person is to help you understand the culture. They should be feel comfortable with asking any questions that come to mind.

Mood Tracker

A mood tracker is part of your planner that allows you to track whether you are feeling happy, sad, tired, angry, bored, etc.

- Blue- Sad
- Red- Angry
- Yellow – Happy
- Green- Anxious
- Orange- Worried
- Purple- Scared

Add your own code

Reflection Introduction

Have you ever felt isolated by the uniqueness of your story, as though not many people truly understand your journey? If you've experienced the life of a Third Culture Kid (TCK), you know the profound value of being recognized and understood within your differences.

As you finish your high schooling, we hope this journey equips you with the tools you need for the next destination in your life. The reflections in this section focus on experiences shared by most TCKs, reminding you that you are not alone in your journey. Together, we can embrace our unique stories and find strength in our shared experiences

The River

The River: Your Self-Reflection Tool
The river is a powerful tool you'll use throughout the planner. It serves as your processing and self-reflection tool, helping you assess where you are in your journey and how you are coping along the way.

Imagine one side of the river represents your current location, and the other side represents your destination—this could be your passport country. The river itself is where you process your transition.

Within this metaphorical river, you might sometimes feel like you're drowning. Reflect on the supports that are helping you stay afloat. Ask yourself:
• What supports are keeping me up?
• Do I feel like I'm still in the middle of the river, or have I reached the shore?

Using the river as a visualization tool can help you navigate the complexities of your transition and provide a clearer perspective on your progress and well-being.

Donovan (1991) A model of major transition

NOTES:

Important dates & Birthdays

Contacts

Name	Socials	Phone

12 Months Ahead

Practical

THINK
- What are you planning for the coming year?
- Do you need to apply for scholarships?
- Is there financial aid available for you?
- Do you need to learn to cook or clean?

DECIDE
- Who is your bridging person?
- What meals do you want to learn to cook?

Heart

SHARE
- How do you feel about leaving?
- How do you feel about where you are going?
- What are you concerned about?
- What are you looking forward to?

DISCUSS
- What do you want to do before you go?
- Who do you want to spend your final year with?

TO DO:
- ☐
- ☐
- ☐
- ☐
- ☐
- ☐
- ☐

MOOD TRACKER
- ☐ Week 1
- ☐ Week 2
- ☐ Week 3
- ☐ Week 4
- ☐ Week 5
- ☐ Week 6
- ☐ Week 7
- ☐ Week 8
- ☐ Week 9
- ☐ Week 10
- ☐ Week 11
- ☐ Week 12

THOUGHTS AND PLANS

REFLECTION

What is a TCK?
Have you ever heard of the term TCK? It stands for Third Culture Kid, which refers to someone who has spent a significant part of their developmental years living outside their parents' culture. This unique experience often leads to greater cultural awareness compared to their peers who grow up in a single culture. TCKs typically have a deeper understanding of diverse perspectives. However, they may also experience a sense of not fully belonging in either their passport country or their current country of residence.

Am I a TCK?
Reflecting on your experience can help you understand whether you are a TCK. Every person's journey is unique, and everyone brings their own strengths that they develop along the way. If you're unsure or would like more input, you can visit VIA Character Strengths and take the free survey.

Self-Reflection Questions
•Were the results what I was expecting?

•What are the things I appreciate about myself? These are moments when I have been proud of myself.

•What strengths do I see in myself?

•How have I seen my strengths play out in my journey?

•Taking time to reflect on these questions can provide valuable insights into your identity and help you appreciate the unique aspects of your journey.

QUESTIONS TO PONDER

•What kind of feelings have come to the surface when I think about my strengths?

•Do I have a positive view of myself and my character?

•Is what I expect of myself reasonable and realistic?

NOTES:

Photo Scavenger Hunt

INSTRUCTIONS:
Photo scavenger hunts are a fun way to revisit favourite spots and dwell literally or mentally on important memories. You can do this hunt all together as a group of friends or split into teams or with your family and make it a little more competitive. Either way, it's best to give yourself a time limit and an idea of what you will do at the end (e.g.. go out to eat, get ice-cream and review the pictures at home, etc.).

A FEW RULES:
Don't take the prompts literally. You can take photos in spots that remind you of the memory in the prompt it doesn't have to be the actual place. You can walk or drive but, if possible, take each photo in a different place.
- You can take selfies, ask other people to be in the photo or ask other people to take the photo for you.
- You should take each photo as a group.
- It's best to stage a scene in each photo to remind you of what you did or felt during this memory. Each person can play themselves or you can switch roles (e.g. If you remember going bungee jumping you might pose yourselves screaming as you pretend to fly through the air over a creek).
- You can hash-tag us #interwoven so we can see the experience

TAKE A PHOTO THAT REMINDS YOU OF:

- A fun holiday you took together.
- Something you did that you never want to do again.
- A memorable airport experience.
- The first place you lived overseas as a family.
- A favourite restaurant.
- Your most interesting food experience.
- A place that amazed you.
- The first place you met some close friends.
- A weird place or experience you never want to forget.
- A place you always wanted to go but never had the chance.
- A really great time with friends.
- A happy reunion.
- A disgusting experience.
- Something embarrassing.
- A time you felt close.
- A favourite cultural experience.
- A time you got a big surprise.
- A time when someone had to go to the hospital.
- Something funny that happened overseas.
- A family disaster.
- A place that feels safe.
- The transport you were on

Pictures of where you live

9 Months Ahead

Practical

THINK
- ☐ What do you want to take with you and what do you want to leave behind?
- ☐ Make a list of your favourite places.
- ☐ What are your travel arrangements?

DECIDE
- ☐ What do you want to have memories of?

Heart

SHARE
- ☐ How do you feel about leaving?
- ☐ How do you feel about where you are going?
- ☐ What are you concerned about?
- ☐ What are you looking forward to?

DISCUSS
- ☐ What are some of the things you would like to do when you enter your new country?

TO DO:
- ☐
- ☐
- ☐
- ☐
- ☐
- ☐
- ☐

MOOD TRACKER
- ☐ Week 1
- ☐ Week 2
- ☐ Week 3
- ☐ Week 4
- ☐ Week 5
- ☐ Week 6
- ☐ Week 7
- ☐ Week 8
- ☐ Week 9
- ☐ Week 10
- ☐ Week 11
- ☐ Week 12

THOUGHTS AND PLANS

REFLECTION

Seeking Feedback from Others
In the previous reflection section, I focused on identifying my own strengths. Now, it's time to gather insights from those who know me well.

Ask My Best Friend:
- What strengths do you see in me?

- How have you seen these strengths influence my life?

Ask a Parent:
- What strengths have you observed developing in me?

- How have you seen me grow?

Ask an Adult I Respect:
- What strengths do you see in me?

- How do you think I can further develop these strengths?

QUESTIONS TO PONDER

- Do I see the same things in myself as others see in me?

- Does it feel like those around me know me?

-
- What strengths do I want people to see in me?

NOTES:

Pictures of your favourite restaurants

Pictures of important people in your life

6 Months Ahead

Practical

THINK
- ☐ What will you do in an emergency?
- ☐ Make a list of people with whom you want to spend time before you go.
- ☐ What are some habits you can start now to have family connection?

DECIDE
- ☐ Are all your travel documents up to date?
- ☐ What documents do you need to take with you? E.g. birth certificates, ID papers
- ☐ Make a travel pack

Heart

SHARE
- ☐ How do you feel about leaving?
- ☐ How do you feel about where you are going?
- ☐ What are you concerned about?
- ☐ What are you looking forward to?

DISCUSS
- ☐ What do you want to do before you go?
- ☐ What does your family think about your plan?

TO DO:
- ☐
- ☐
- ☐
- ☐
- ☐
- ☐

MOOD TRACKER
- ☐ Week 1
- ☐ Week 2
- ☐ Week 3
- ☐ Week 4
- ☐ Week 5
- ☐ Week 6
- ☐ Week 7
- ☐ Week 8
- ☐ Week 9
- ☐ Week 10
- ☐ Week 11
- ☐ Week 12

THOUGHTS AND PLANS

REFLECTION

The places and people we experience in our lives leave their mark. Like colours that change the landscape of our experience. There is both beauty and struggle in every context and culture. Some of these struggles can be difficult to comprehend, especially as you navigate the highs and lows of life.

- What are some examples of the beauty that I have experienced and seen in the places I have lived?

- What are the things I appreciate most about my current context and the journey I have been on?

- What are some of the things I have experienced in my current culture that I value and would like to carry with me into my future cultural context?

- What are the things that have become a part of me that I want people to understand?

QUESTIONS TO PONDER

- Are there things I have learned that those who only live in one culture might miss?

- What are the things I really wish people knew about my experience when they meet me?

- Are there things I see in my cultural experience that don't really line up with any of the cultures I have lived in?

NOTES:

Write out your favourite phrases or slang from your country

Pictures of your favourite spots

3 Months Ahead

Practical

THINK
- [ ] What do you plan to do for income?
- [ ] Start planning days with special people in your life.
- [ ] Are there people with whom you need to reconcile?

DECIDE
- [ ] Who can write a reference for future employment?
- [ ] Start sorting what you will take with you and what you will leave behind.
- [ ] Do you need to purchase gifts to take with you?

Heart

SHARE
- [ ] How do you feel about leaving?
- [ ] How do you feel about where you are going?
- [ ] What are you concerned about?
- [ ] What are you looking forward to?

DISCUSS
- [ ] How will you continue your friendships through this transition?
- [ ] How will you keep in contact?

TO DO:
- [ ]
- [ ]
- [ ]
- [ ]
- [ ]
- [ ]

MOOD TRACKER
- [ ] Week 1
- [ ] Week 2
- [ ] Week 3
- [ ] Week 4

THOUGHTS AND PLANS

REFLECTION

Life is a mix of the good and the bad, the joyful and difficult and everything in between. It can be difficult to find a place to share the hard parts of being a global resident. So start here.

- What are the things I have experienced that are hard to share?

- Are there things in my current cultural context that I am looking forward to leaving behind?

- What are the things that I see in my community that I don't want to continue in my own life?

- What are some of the cultural norms I have noticed in any of my contexts of experience?

QUESTIONS TO PONDER

- How have I handled the parts of culture that aren't beautiful through different stages of my life and in different locations?

- How do I share my concerns about unhealthy cultural norms in a way that will be heard?

- Who would be a good person to process these thoughts with?

NOTES:

Make a packaging collage of your favourite labels

Recipes of your favourite food

2 Months Ahead

Practical

THINK
- ☐ Who do you want to be present for your departure and arrival?
- ☐ What will you use for transport at your new location?
- ☐ What practical gear will you need at your new place?

DECIDE
- ☐ How do you want to say goodbye? E.g. party, event,
- ☐ Plan your goodbyes.

Heart

SHARE
- ☐ How do you feel about leaving?
- ☐ How do you feel about where you are going?
- ☐ What are you concerned about?
- ☐ What are you looking forward to?

DISCUSS
- ☐ How do you say, "No," in a culturally appropriate way?
- ☐ What are some boundaries you have established that you want to keep as you move?
- ☐ Mark where you sit currently on the river diagram.

TO DO:
- ☐
- ☐
- ☐
- ☐
- ☐
- ☐
- ☐

MOOD TRACKER
- ☐ Week 1
- ☐ Week 2
- ☐ Week 3
- ☐ Week 4

THOUGHTS AND PLANS

REFLECTION

Everything is about to change. This could be exciting, terrifying, or a mix of both with many other emotions thrown in. Whether I feel prepared or completely out of my depth, it's okay to be where I am and feel what I feel. There is no right way to navigate or feel about this kind of life change.

How can I maintain and nurture the relationships that matter to me through these changes?

Who are the people I want to maintain connection with through my next season?

What kinds of things can I do to build up the connection before we part ways?
- Make a plan for communication (i.e. regular video call, ongoing group chat, online gaming times, letter writing)
- Set expectations together. - talk about what you are hoping will happen in the **coming weeks** and beyond.
- Plan a meet up - if possible set a time in the future to get together again.

QUESTIONS TO PONDER

• How much time can I invest in carrying relationships forward when I will be building new relationships as well?

• Who are the people that I know I can pick up where I left off with? Even when we have been apart or out of touch for a long time I am able to reconnect well.

NOTES:

Countries

```
M C G V A O C T T M V I E T N A M Z
N N A E M U A A P A K Q S A U W B C
T E E N R Q X N M L A A Z U S Z R A
K H W P A M Q Z X A Z D E S A W A M
T F A Z A D A A O Y A E T T X R Z B
K H P I E L A N Z S K N H R C D I O
R E C E L A T I Y I H G I A I K L D
Y P N H R A L A H A S L O L F O U I
D U Y Y I U N A L A T A P I J J S A
I N D I A N T D N D A N I A G C A B
J M O B S Y A J L D N D A I H U L Q
W Q E Z W U U C R Q G B J A K Q Q Y
```

Find the following words in the puzzle.
Words are hidden → ↓ and ↘ .

NEW ZEALAND   CAMBODIA   KENYA
KAZAKHSTAN   VIETNAM   NEPAL
AUSTRALIA   ENGLAND   INDIA
ETHIOPIA   GERMANY   PERU
TANZANIA   BRAZIL   USA
THAILAND   CANADA
MALAYSIA   CHINA

Pictures of your friends

1 Month Ahead

Practical

THINK
- ☐ Make a list of the things you want to do in the first week after you arrive.
- ☐ What are the cultural norms in the place to which you are moving?
- ☐ What are the road safety rules?

DECIDE
- ☐ Are there still goodbyes you want to say?
- ☐ Make a plan for emergency situations.
- ☐ Is there anything you want to take back with you that you need to buy?

Heart

SHARE
- ☐ What are the emotions you are feeling at this moment?
- ☐ Is there anything you are concerned about?
- ☐ What are you looking forward to?

DISCUSS
- ☐ Make a goal list for your life transition?
- ☐ What is your plan for maintaining boundaries?

TO DO:
- ☐
- ☐
- ☐
- ☐
- ☐
- ☐
- ☐

MOOD TRACKER
- ☐ Week 1
- ☐ Week 2
- ☐ Week 3
- ☐ Week 4

THOUGHTS AND PLANS

REFLECTION

Are there things I am looking forward to leaving behind? The weather, food options, difficult relationships, cultural expectations, challenging stages of life? Its OK to be ready to leave things behind and to be hopeful when looking forward. Hope and grief can live in the same space. That is the beauty of being human.

•I am ready to leave these things behind:

•I am relieved to be moving on from:

•I am giving myself permission the grieve these things:

•I am giving myself permission to be excited about and enjoy these things:

QUESTIONS TO PONDER

•Are there feelings that I am experiencing that I feel guilty about? Does that come from my own expectations for how this process should work or from others?

•Do I really believe that it is ok to feel what I feel and let myself sit with my experience before I decide if it is something I need to act on or not?

NOTES:

A copy of currency

Pictures of iconic/comical signs/ Cultural things

1 Week Ahead

Practical

THINK
- [ ] What do you need to do in the last week?
- [ ] Who are the people to whom you need to say goodbye?
- [ ] Make a list of things to pack.

DECIDE
- [ ] Start packing, weigh your luggage.
- [ ] What is the last meal you want to eat?

Heart

SHARE
- [ ] Breathe.
- [ ] How are you feeling?
- [ ] What are you concerned about?
- [ ] What are you looking forward to?

DISCUSS
- [ ] What have been your best memories in this location?
- [ ] What treasures are you taking with you?

TO DO:
- [ ]
- [ ]
- [ ]
- [ ]
- [ ]
- [ ]
- [ ]

MOOD TRACKER
- [ ] Day 1
- [ ] Day 2
- [ ] Day 3
- [ ] Day 4
- [ ] Day 5
- [ ] Day 6
- [ ] Day 7

THOUGHTS AND PLANS

REFLECTION

The time is coming up so fast, can you believe this year has flown by or has it ? This is your last week before traveling. There must be so many emotions going through your mind and heart at this time. Breathe- cause we often forget to breathe. Use your five senses and take them in. Smell the smells, touch the things, Eat the food and hug the people. But most of all enjoy this time.

• What are the things I have loved most about this week ?

• How have I cared for myself while preparing to leave ?

QUESTIONS TO PONDER

• What are things I haven't had the chance to process in this time ?

• When can I make time to process?

NOTES:

Create a map of where you currently live ?

Collect photos of the people you want to remember & write what you value about this person.

Travel

REFLECTION

The time is coming up so fast, can you believe this year has flown by or has it ? This is your last week before traveling. There must be so many emotions going through your mind and heart at this time. Breathe- cause we often forget to breathe. Use your five senses and take them in. Smell the smells, touch the things, Eat the food and hug the people. But most of all enjoy this time.

- What are the things I have loved most about this week ?

- How have I cared for myself while preparing to leave ?

MOOD TRACKER

☐ Day 1

☐ Day 2

☐ Day 3

☐ Day 4

☐ Day 5

☐ Day 6

☐ Day 7

THOUGHTS AND PLANS

1 Week After

Practical

THINK
- ☐ Take time to adjust. Give yourself grace and know your boundaries.
- ☐ Talk to your bridging person.
- ☐ What routines do you want in your life? E.g. meals, exercise, church

DECIDE
- ☐ Do you need a driver's licence?
- ☐ Do you need to set up communications? E.g. phone, internet

Heart

SHARE
- ☐ What have you enjoyed so far?
- ☐ What has been the hardest part?
- ☐ What are you looking forward to?

DISCUSS
- ☐ What are you missing?
- ☐ How is the jet-lag effecting you?
- ☐ Mark where you sit currently on the river diagram.

TO DO:
- ☐
- ☐
- ☐
- ☐
- ☐
- ☐
- ☐

MOOD TRACKER
- ☐ Day 1
- ☐ Day 2
- ☐ Day 3
- ☐ Day 4
- ☐ Day 5
- ☐ Day 6
- ☐ Day 7

THOUGHTS AND PLANS

REFLECTION

Feeling overwhelmed after a challenging week? Adjusting to new environments or re-acclimating to familiar ones can be taxing, especially when dealing with jet lag and other stresses. It's important to acknowledge that you may not have the capacity for in-depth thinking at the moment—and that's completely fine.

Whether you're encountering new experiences, sights, and smells, or returning to the familiar comforts and challenges of a place you know, it's natural to feel a mix of emotions. The Third Culture Kid (TCK) life often embodies this duality—balancing both new and old. Remember, adjusting takes time, and you've only been back for a week. Give yourself the grace to ease in.

QUESTIONS

- What are some of the new or old things in life you are adjusting to ?

NOTES:

1 Month After

Practical

THINK
- ☐ What things can you do to get to know this place?
- ☐ With whom you are connecting?
- ☐ What church do you want to be part of?

DECIDE
- ☐ What can you do to start making friends and find new activities?
- ☐ Do you need to write a resume?

Heart

SHARE
- ☐ What have you enjoyed so far?
- ☐ What are you missing?
- ☐ What has been the hardest part?
- ☐ Have you been able to share your story?

DISCUSS
- ☐ How has sharing your story affected you?
- ☐ What expectations are you bringing with your from your previous context?

TO DO:
- ☐
- ☐
- ☐
- ☐
- ☐
- ☐
- ☐

MOOD TRACKER
- ☐ Week 1
- ☐ Week 2
- ☐ Week 3
- ☐ Week 4
- ☐ Week 5
- ☐ Week 6
- ☐ Week 7
- ☐ Week 8

THOUGHTS AND PLANS

REFLECTION

Reflecting on your return to your host country, what aspects of your life have been easy to adjust to, and what challenges are you facing? You've been back for a month now and might have started learning to drive, job hunting, or beginning university. These are significant steps that naturally require time and patience.

It's understandable to miss the simplicity of your previous life.
Have you allowed yourself the grace to take things one step at a time? Creating a plan for your next steps can help manage the transition. For example, building new friendships can be a gradual process, often requiring about 10 hours to form meaningful connections.

While Third Culture Kids (TCKs) might prefer deep connections right away, it's important to remember that in some cultures, people might take a different approach, seeming reserved but genuinely wanting to know you in their own way.

QUESTION TO PONDER

What relationships would you like to deepen?

Think about the connections that are meaningful to you. Are there specific friends, family members, or colleagues you want to get closer to?

Discomfort in Building Relationships:

Are there aspects of relationship building in your new setting that make you feel uneasy? Identify these areas to understand what might be hindering your connections.

Disruptive Expectations:

Reflect on the expectations you have for your relationships and interactions. Are these expectations realistic, or are they causing discomfort and disruption? Consider how these expectations might be impacting your ability to build deeper relationships

NOTES:

Wreck this page

Photos of family before and after

3 Months After

Practical

THINK
- ☐ How well are you connecting with people?
- ☐ What new activities have you found?

DECIDE
- ☐ How ready are you to invest in new relationships?
- ☐ Is your financial plan working?

Heart

SHARE
- ☐ What is the best thing so far?
- ☐ What has been the hardest thing so far?
- ☐ What are you looking forward to?
- ☐ What are you missing?

DISCUSS
- ☐ What has surprised you since moving?
- ☐ What has matched your expectations?

TO DO:
- ☐
- ☐
- ☐
- ☐
- ☐
- ☐

Mood Tracker
- ☐ Week 1
- ☐ Week 2
- ☐ Week 3
- ☐ Week 4
- ☐ Week 5
- ☐ Week 6
- ☐ Week 7
- ☐ Week 8
- ☐ Week 9
- ☐ Week 10
- ☐ Week 11
- ☐ Week 12

THOUGHTS AND PLANS

REFLECTION

It has been three months since you moved into your new place. How are you adjusting? Have there been any surprising or frustrating experiences? What were some things you did not anticipate—both internally and externally?

By now, you may have begun to find a rhythm and routine to help you acclimate to your new surroundings. Often, around this time, you might start to feel more comfortable: not getting lost, establishing a routine, and expanding your social circle. If this hasn't happened yet, have you considered starting a new hobby? What are your interests? Is there a local group you could join? Connecting with people who share similar interests is essential for building meaningful relationships.

This period typically involves a blend of excitement, challenges, and gradual adaptation as you readjust to life in your new environment. It's crucial to be patient and give yourself the time needed to navigate this complex emotional journey.
How have you found your experience so far?

QUESTION TO PONDER

• What are two activities you have done or can do this week to help you feel more connected and settled in your current location?

NOTES:

Create a map of your new location

Photos of life at the moment and how you feel about it.

6 Months After

Practical

THINK
- [ ] What have been worthwhile activities since you arrived?
- [ ] Do you have quality people around you?
- [ ] Are you enjoying yourself?
- [ ] What is your spiritual life like?

DECIDE
- [ ] Are there any changes you need to make to your current habits?
- [ ] Are there new things you want to start?

Heart

SHARE
- [ ] What is the best thing so far?
- [ ] What has been the hardest thing so far?
- [ ] What are you looking forward to?
- [ ] What are you missing?

DISCUSS
- [ ] Mark where you currently sit on the river diagram.
- [ ] How are you doing with the move?

TO DO:
- [ ]
- [ ]
- [ ]
- [ ]
- [ ]
- [ ]
- [ ]

MOOD TRACKER
- [ ] Week 1
- [ ] Week 2
- [ ] Week 3
- [ ] Week 4
- [ ] Week 5
- [ ] Week 6
- [ ] Week 7
- [ ] Week 8
- [ ] Week 9
- [ ] Week 10
- [ ] Week 11
- [ ] Week 12

THOUGHTS AND PLANS

REFLECTION

It's been six months since you left the place you once called home. The honeymoon period might be over—is that how it feels to you? Have some of the initial novelties worn off? Have you found your community yet? This phase can often be the most challenging, where feelings of homesickness, unfulfilled new connections, and the fading of old relationships become more pronounced. If this resonates with you, know that you are not alone.

- Are there unexpected things you find yourself grieving?

- Have you had an opportunity to debrief?

QUESTIONS TO PONDER:

- Who in your life can you talk to about this process?

- Would you benefit from formal debriefing?

For more information, check out what debriefing means on our resource page.

NOTES:

Favourite new restaurants and food

Wreck this page

9 Months After

Practical

THINK
- ☐ Where do you have input into your community?
- ☐ Who are your support people?

DECIDE
- ☐ To what degree can you invest in your friends from your previous location?
- ☐ Do you need more supportive people close to you?

Heart

SHARE
- ☐ What is the best thing so far?
- ☐ What has been the hardest thing so far?
- ☐ What are you looking forward to?
- ☐ What are you missing?

DISCUSS
- ☐ Where is your heart?
- ☐ What can you contribute to the place in which you are now living?
- ☐ What do you want out of the place in which you are now living?

TO DO:
- ☐
- ☐
- ☐
- ☐
- ☐
- ☐
- ☐
- ☐

MOOD TRACKER
- ☐ Week 1
- ☐ Week 2
- ☐ Week 3
- ☐ Week 4
- ☐ Week 5
- ☐ Week 6
- ☐ Week 7
- ☐ Week 8
- ☐ Week 9
- ☐ Week 10
- ☐ Week 11
- ☐ Week 12

THOUGHTS AND PLANS

REFLECTION

Breathe. Take a moment to reflect on how far you've come. The past 21 months have been a whirlwind of growth and change, regardless of your age. It's been a roller coaster, filled with both joys and challenges. Have you had the chance to share your journey with those in your new circle?

Sharing your story can be like enjoying a bowl of ice cream—some people only want the toppings, while others may not understand the full experience, like those who visit a country but never live there. Occasionally, you meet someone who truly gets it, and you don't have to explain yourself.

No matter how your journey has unfolded, take a breath and look around. There is no right or wrong way to navigate this path.

QUESTIONS TO PONDER:

- What changes have you noticed in yourself? What has remained the same?

- Have you found yourself frustrated with people who don't share your values?

NOTES:

Design by Zeborah Grace

Wreck this page

12 Months After

Practical

THINK
- ☐ How do you feel about the journey you have been on?
- ☐ Do you feel connected to this community?

DECIDE
- ☐ Are there changes you need to make?
- ☐ What is your plan for making those changes?

Heart

SHARE
- ☐ What is the best thing so far?
- ☐ What has been the hardest thing so far?
- ☐ What are you looking forward to?
- ☐ What are you missing?

DISCUSS
- ☐ Talk with someone about what these 24 months have been like.
- ☐ Mark where you sit on the river diagram.
- ☐ How do you see yourself within your community?

TO DO:
- ☐
- ☐
- ☐
- ☐
- ☐
- ☐
- ☐

MOOD TRACKER
- ☐ Week 1
- ☐ Week 2
- ☐ Week 3
- ☐ Week 4
- ☐ Week 5
- ☐ Week 6
- ☐ Week 7
- ☐ Week 8
- ☐ Week 9
- ☐ Week 10
- ☐ Week 11
- ☐ Week 12

THOUGHTS AND PLANS

REFLECTION

It's been a year—what an incredible milestone! Reflect on the significant changes you've experienced this past year. Are there aspects of your life that once held great importance but now seem less significant? Conversely, have things that once seemed trivial taken on new meaning?

Looking back over the last two years, how has your understanding of transformation evolved? What insights do you now possess that you wish you could have shared with your past self when you began this journey?

Take some time to share these reflections with a friend. Remember, growth is not a straight line; it's a winding path where encouragement is essential. This is just one season of your journey, and so much more awaits you.

May your heart and mind remain open and ready to learn and transform, as you inspire others along the way. Thank you for journeying with us. We're here for you, so feel free to reach out and share your experiences.

Cheers to your continued growth and adventure.

NOTES:

Favourite new phrases and slang

Favourite places

Glossary

USE THIS TO WRITE YOUR OWN LANGUAGE FAVOURITE WORDS AND MEANINGS WITH YOUR FRIENDS AND FAMILY.

Resources

BOOKS

- Misunderstood: The Impact of Growing Up Overseas in the 21st Century – Tanya Crossman (Summertime Publishing, 2016).
- Third Culture Kids: Growing Up Among Worlds (3rd Edition) – David Pollock, Ruth Van Reken, Michael Pollock (Nicholas Brealey Publishing, 2017).
- Belonging Everywhere and Nowhere: Insights into Counselling the Globally Mobile – Lois Bushong (Mango Tree Intercultural Services, 2013).
- Third Culture Kids: A Gift to Care For – Ulrika Ernvik (Familjeglädje, 2018).
- Expat Teens Talk: Peers, Parents and Professionals offer support, advice and solutions in response to Expat Life challenges as shared by Expat Teens – Lisa Pittman and Diana Smit (Summertime Publishing, 2012).
- The Global Nomad's Guide to University Transition, 2nd Ed. – Tina Quick (Tina L Quick, 2022).
- The Re-entry Roadmap: Find Your Best Next Step After Living Abroad – Cate Brubaker (Thinking Travel Press, 2018).
- Arriving Well – Cate Brubaker, Doreen Cumberford, Helen Watts (Kindle Direct Publishing, 2018).
- The Art of Coming Home – Craig Storti (Nicholas Brealey Publishing, 2001).
- Looming Transitions – Amy Young (CreateSpace Independent Publishing Platform, 2015).
- Returning Well: Your Guide to Thriving Back "Home" After Serving Cross-Culturally – Melissa Chaplin (Newton Publishers, 2015).
- Burn-Up or Splash Down: surviving the culture shock of re-entry – Marion Knell (IVP Books, 2007).
- Re-Entry: Making The Transition From Missions To Life At Home – Peter Jordan (YWAM, 2013).
- Unstacking Your Grief Tower – Lauren Wells (Independently published, 2021).
- Belonging Beyond Borders – Megan Norton (Belonging Beyond Borders LLC, 2022).
- Between Worlds: Essays on Culture and Belonging – Marilyn Gardner (Doorlight Publications, 2015).
- Worlds Apart: A Third Culture Kid's Journey – Marilyn Gardner (Doorlight Publications, 2018)

Debriefing

Debriefing is a structured process of reflecting on and discussing experiences, typically following a significant event or period of time. It involves unpacking what happened, understanding the emotions and reactions involved, and drawing lessons from the experience.

In the context of TCKs (Third Culture Kids) or anyone going through significant life transitions, debriefing can be especially valuable. It helps individuals make sense of their experiences, process any grief or loss, and gain insights that can aid in their personal growth and adaptation to new environments.

By engaging in debriefing, you can clarify your thoughts, feelings, and memories, allowing you to move forward with greater understanding and resilience.

If you are interested in debriefing, here are some places to contact:

- Interwoven offers debriefings for singles and families in Australia.
- TCK Training offers debriefs.
- Resource: Unpacking Your Grief Tower is a great resource to explore by yourself.